NATURE'S NINJA

ANIMALS WITH SPECTACULAR SKILLS

REBECCA L. JOHNSON

M Millbrook Press • Minneapolis

For Beth, Val, and Kristin—my writing sisters. Thanks for all the years of support, encouragement, and laughter.

Text copyright © 2020 by Rebecca L. Johnson

Millbrook Press
An imprint of Lerner Publishing Group, Inc.
241 First Avenue North
Minneapolis, MN 55401 USA

For reading levels and more information, look up this title at www.lernerbooks.com.

Main body text set in Caecilia LT Std.
Typeface provided by Adobe Systems.

Library of Congress Cataloging-in-Publication Data

Names: Johnson, Rebecca L., author.
Title: Nature's ninja : animals with spectacular skills / Rebecca L. Johnson.
Description: Minneapolis : Millbrook Press, [2020] | Audience: Age 10–14. | Audience: Grade 4 to 6.
    | Includes bibliographical references and index.
Identifiers: LCCN 2018047662 (print) | LCCN 2018048346 (ebook) | ISBN 9781541562615 (eb pdf) |
    ISBN 9781541542419 (lb : alk. paper)
Subjects: LCSH: Animals—Juvenile literature. | Animal behavior—Juvenile literature. | Animal
    attacks—Juvenile literature. | Animal defenses—Juvenile literature.
Classification: LCC QL49 (ebook) | LCC QL49 .J628 2020 (print) | DDC 591.47—dc23

LC record available at https://lccn.loc.gov/2018047662

Manufactured in the United States of America
1-45408-39521-3/21/2019

CONTENTS

THE ART of THE NINJA

Two guards stand beneath flickering torches outside the commander's house.
Three others patrol the walled courtyard. All are ready to draw their swords at the slightest noise.

But the man on the roof doesn't make a sound. Dressed in dark clothing from head to toe, he grips the roof's edge and swings, like an acrobat, into an open window. Moments later, he emerges with maps of his enemy's positions secured beneath his shirt.

He drops silently to the ground and waits for the closest guard to pass. Then he sprints through the shadows toward the wall.

But another guard spots the movement. His cry rings out across the courtyard: "NINJA!"

The guards close in. The ninja levels one with a jumping kick and another with a lightning-fast jab. He blocks a third guard's sword thrust and shoves him into the remaining two. Before the guards can recover, the ninja scales the wall and disappears into the night.

NINJA were legendary warriors in medieval Japan. They were masters of stealth and experts in martial arts. They wielded fearsome weapons and outsmarted their opponents with clever disguises, distractions, and tricks. Learning ninja skills took years of training and practice. Together, those skills were called ninjutsu, or "the art of the ninja."

You've probably seen ninja in movies, comics, and video games. But did you know that you can spot ninja in nature too? These ninja dress in scales, spines, and exoskeletons. They soar, swim, and scramble through environments ranging from shadowy forests to sunlit seas. And their spectacular skills rival those of the greatest ninjutsu masters.

To find these animal ninja, though, you must know where to look.

This nineteenth-century woodcut shows a sword-wielding Japanese warrior trained in ninjutsu.

CHAPTER 1

TOEHOLDS

Momentarily airborne, a gargoyle gecko (Rhacodactylus auriculatus) executes a ninja-worthy leap.

NINJA SKILL

SHINOBI-IRI

ABLE TO WALK AND RUN SILENTLY, ENTER BUILDINGS AND CAMPS UNDETECTED, AND CLIMB, LEAP, AND TUMBLE LIKE AN ACROBAT

A gecko grips the trunk of a tree near an open window. Inside the house, a ceiling light is on. Moths circle its warm glow.

The gecko leaps onto the windowpane, its feet sticking instantly to the glass.

Silently, the little lizard slips into the house. It scales the smooth white walls and scampers across the glossy ceiling.

It hangs upside down by its toes near the light, waiting for the moths to flutter within reach.

Ninja warriors were greatly feared—and admired—for their ability to walk and run without making a sound, leap like acrobats, and climb with almost superhuman agility and speed.

Geckos have them beat.

These lizards may be nature's most skilled climbers. In tropical regions worldwide, they often silently slip into buildings, run up walls, and scurry across ceilings as they hunt insect prey. Geckos are famous for their ability to cling to any surface, including smooth metal and glass, whether right side up or upside down.

For centuries, people puzzled over how geckos climb and cling like they do. Research revealed that the secret isn't a sticky glue. Gecko toes are dry and silky smooth. It also isn't itty-bitty suction cups, static electricity, or something like Velcro.

The gecko's *shinobi-iri* secret is tiny hairs. Billions of them.

THE SCIENCE BEHIND THE STORY

Geckos have five toes on each foot. Small, flexible ridges cover the underside of each toe (the toe pad). These ridges are made up of millions of microscopic hairs, or setae (SEE-tee). At their tips, setae split into hundreds of much finer hairlike structures called spatulae (SPAH-tchoo-lee). All told, the average gecko has about two billion spatulae on its feet.

Spatulae are the key to a gecko's amazing grip. When spatulae contact any surface, they stick to it due to the slight attraction (a tiny pull) between molecules in the spatulae and

Above: A close-up of a gecko's toe pads shows the ridges made up of setae. Below: A high-magnification view of setae. Note how they split into many spatulae at their tips.

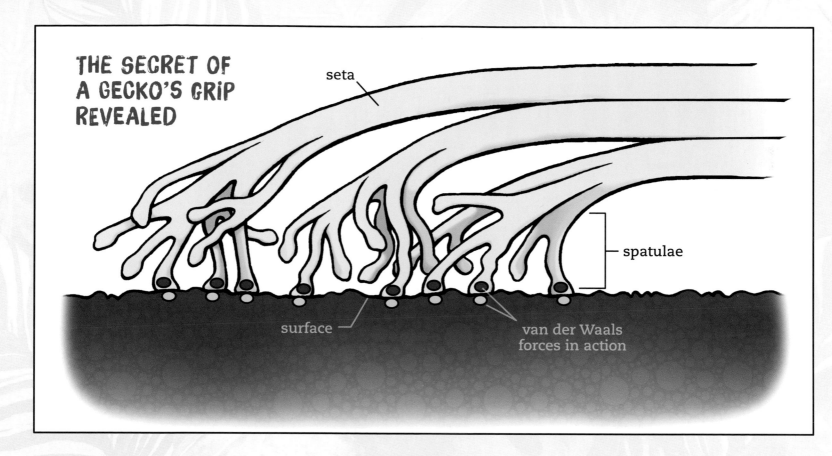

THE SECRET OF
A GECKO'S GRIP
REVEALED

seta

spatulae

surface

van der Waals
forces in action

molecules of what the spatulae are touching. These weak molecular attractions are called van der Waals forces.

The sticking power of a single spatula on a gecko's toe isn't much. But when lots of spatulae work together, the force is remarkably strong.

Scientists have discovered that not only is it easy for geckos to grip something very tightly, but it's also easy for them to let go. Robert Full from the University of California at Berkeley studies how geckos and all sorts of other animals move. Full and his colleagues have shown that to release its

grip, a gecko simply changes the angle at which its spatulae are touching something. A slight shift overcomes the van der Waals forces, and—*presto!*—the spatulae pull free.

A common way for geckos to do this is to curl up their toes (see the photo on page 6). "They have special muscles and tendons on top of their toes that work a bit like puppet strings," said Full. In slow motion, the release looks as if the toes are peeling up from a surface, like you'd peel away a piece of tape. In real time, it happens incredibly fast.

CHAPTER 2

SHOOTING STARS

Armed with sharp spines, a collector sea urchin (Tripneustes gratilla) sits on the ocean floor near the coast of Australia.

NINJA SKILL
SHURIKEN-JUTSU

USING HANDHELD THROWING BLADES, INCLUDING *BOU SHURIKEN* (STRAIGHT SPIKES) AND *SHAKEN* (WHEEL-LIKE THROWING STARS), TO DISABLE OR FEND OFF ATTACKERS

The sea urchin looks like a big pincushion on the ocean floor. Its round body bristles with stiff, pointed spines. The urchin's underside, however, is less protected.

A hungry fish approaches. It bites down on one of the spines and tugs, trying unsuccessfully to flip the urchin over. The fish lets go, slowly circles, and then darts in to try again.

But suddenly the attacker is under attack. Dozens of tiny biting . . . *things* . . . have suddenly appeared in the water around the urchin. Not wanting to risk a face full of pain, the fish flees with a flick of its tail.

All sea urchins have spines to protect against predators. Clustered around the base of the spines are small structures called pedicellariae (peh-dih-seh-LAIR-ee-ee) that look like miniature jaws atop movable stalks. Pedicellariae work to remove sand and tiny organisms that land on or try to attach to an urchin. One type of pedicellaria will also nip at predators trying to push through the urchin's spiny defense.

But collector urchins (*Tripneustes gratilla*) take their defense a step further. They can deploy the biting jaws—the heads—of their nipping pedicellariae like ninja throwing blades.

When harassed, a collector urchin launches dozens, even hundreds, of pedicellaria heads into the surrounding water. These minute snapping structures form a protective cloud around the urchin. Not only will they sink their razor-sharp fangs into any attacker they make contact with, but they'll also inject a painful dose of poison.

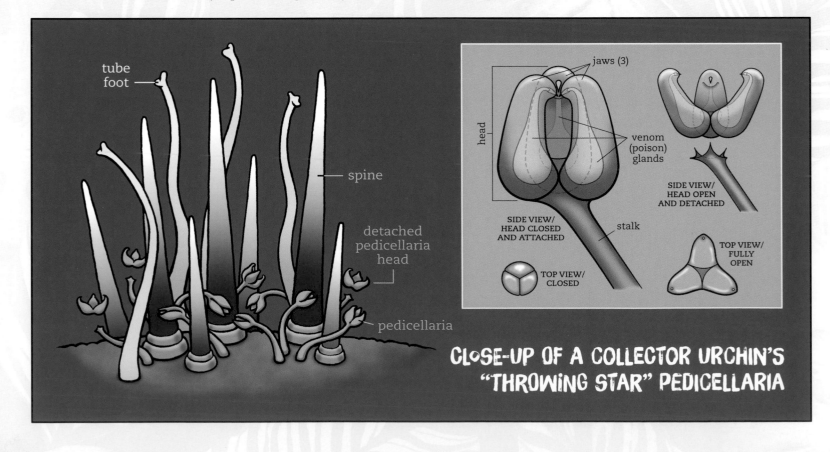

CLOSE-UP OF A COLLECTOR URCHIN'S "THROWING STAR" PEDICELLARIA

An enlarged view of a collector urchin's "throwing stars." The wide-open jaws of these pedicellaria heads will clamp down on whatever they come into contact with.

THE SCIENCE BEHIND THE STORY

Marine ecologist Hannah Sheppard-Brennand recently discovered the collector urchin's *shuriken-jutsu*-like defense. As part of her research at Australia's Southern Cross University, she kept collector urchins in aquariums in her laboratory. Almost every time she touched the spiny animals, she ended up with pedicellaria heads stuck in the skin of her hands. It was more than annoying. The bites hurt and swelled like beestings.

"I wondered whether this release of pedicellaria heads could be in response to the risk of predation," Sheppard-Brennand said. To test this hypothesis, she and her colleagues put collector urchins in small tanks. Then they gently tapped the urchins with forceps to simulate a predator attack.

Within seconds, the urchins began releasing snapping pedicellaria heads into the water around them. "You can see them with the naked eye," Sheppard-Brennand said. "They look like tiny, dark triangles."

Other animals shoot out defensive weapons. Think of a porcupine's quills or an octopus's cloud of ink. But Sheppard-Brennand thinks the collector urchin is special, releasing what she calls semiautonomous venomous devices in response to a threat. In other words, when the pedicellaria heads are released, they work independently from the urchin. "The jaws of the heads open and close repeatedly, perhaps to increase the chances of biting a predator if they come into contact with it," she said.

Somehow, these living "throwing stars" are able to sense their surroundings, sink their fangs into an attacker, and deliver a nasty bite—all on their own.

CHAPTER 3

BLADE RUNNER

An Atlantic sailfish (Istiophorus albicans) works with others of its kind to herd and then attack sardines off Mexico's eastern coast.

NINJA SKILL

KEN-JUTSU

THE ART OF SWORDSMANSHIP;
WIELDING ANY TYPE OF
SWORD WITH LETHAL SPEED
AND PRECISION

The sardines are tired and in trouble. Surrounded by their sailfish pursuers, they huddle together near the ocean's surface, forming a knot of frenzy and fear.

Now a single sailfish approaches. Very slowly, it inserts its long, pointed bill into the school of exhausted little fish. Then it slashes—right, left, and right again. So fast it's just a blur.

Silver scales drift down through the blue water. A dozen sardines are injured in this first attack. And the sailfish are just getting started.

Atlantic sailfish (*Istiophorus albicans*) are impressive in so many ways. For starters, they're big, growing up to 10 feet (3 m) long. They're also fast. Sailfish can tear through the water at speeds of 22 to 34 miles (36 to 54 km) per hour. And a sailfish's spectacular "sail"—its large dorsal (top) fin—runs almost the length of its body.

But the sailfish's bill usually draws the most attention. It is formed from extremely elongated bones in the fish's upper jaw. Somewhat rounded, with a pointed tip, the bill is covered with toothlike bumps.

For many years, people weren't quite sure how sailfish used their bills. One long-held idea was that they use them to stab their prey, like you might stab a piece of steak with a knife. But it turns out that sailfish use their bills like ninja sword masters, with blinding speed and deadly accuracy.

A sailfish is poised to insert its swordlike bill into a tightly packed school of exhausted sardines.

THE SCIENCE BEHIND THE STORY

The proof is in the pictures.

Armed with high-speed video cameras, biologist Alexander Wilson and his colleagues got into the water with Atlantic sailfish off the coast of Mexico. While snorkeling alongside these big predators, the scientists filmed them in action.

Sailfish work together to hunt small fish such as sardines. "It is an amazing experience, actually," Wilson said. "What first appears random or chaotic is actually quite an orderly process, where groups of sailfish will cut off a school of sardines near the seafloor, then push them towards the surface where they can be controlled as a type of bait ball."

Once the sailfish have corralled the sardines, they take turns attacking. The scientists replayed their videos in slow motion to reveal the details of these attacks. Typically, a sailfish swims up and slowly inserts its bill into the bait ball. Then it whips its bill from side to side like a sword, slashing at a speed of about 20 feet (6 m) per second. That's roughly the speed at which the tip of a baseball bat moves when a baseball player swings hard at a pitch.

Each slashing attack injures more sardines, making them easier to catch. A sailfish uses its bill to do this too. It taps an injured sardine with the bill's tip, just hard enough to make the little fish swim out of the bait ball. Then the

Researchers come face to face with hunting sailfish as they film these highly skilled predators attacking their prey.

sailfish swoops in and swallows it whole.

"The turn-taking ensures that all the sailfish get some food and don't injure each other by making a mad dash at the sardines at once," Wilson said. The sailfish keep slashing and tapping—and eating—until the last little fish is gone.

CHAPTER 4

BASIC TRAINING

An alkali fly (Ephydra hians) stays safe and dry inside a protective bubble while underwater.

NINJA SKILL

SUIREN-JUTSU

WATER SKILLS, INCLUDING SWIMMING SILENTLY AND USING INGENIOUS DEVICES TO CROSS LAKES AND RIVERS AND TO BREATHE UNDERWATER

It's a small fly. Smaller than a kernel of corn. So small that when it lands on the lake, its feet make only the slightest dimples in the water's surface.

For most living things, diving into this particular lake would be suicide.

Not so for this fly. Headfirst, it takes the plunge. As it pushes beneath the water's surface, it creates a custom-made bubble suit—a protective air submarine—in which it can safely descend.

Ninja invented clever ways to cross bodies of water and to stay submerged for long periods. For example, one *suiren-jutsu* strategy for hiding from enemies was to lie on the bottom of a shallow lake and breathe through a hollow tube. The tube stuck up above the water like a snorkel.

The alkali fly (*Ephydra hians*) has a ninja-worthy trick for spending time underwater in lakes where few living things can survive. Mono Lake in California is one such alkali lake. It is full of chemicals washed down from the surrounding hillsides that make the lake water very alkaline, or basic (the opposite of acidic). The water is also three times saltier than the ocean.

For hundreds of years, people have watched alkali flies dive into Mono Lake, crawl around underwater, and then emerge completely dry. It wasn't until scientists took a closer look, though, that the details of the alkali fly's *suiren-jutsu* secret were revealed.

THE SCIENCE BEHIND THE STORY

To figure out how alkali flies can do what they do, insect experts Floris van Breugel and Michael Dickinson from the California Institute of Technology first had to catch some. Actually, that

Jagged formations of a rocky substance called tufa rise up from the alkaline waters of Mono Lake in California.

step was pretty easy. In late summer, the shores of Mono Lake teem with millions of alkali flies. They come to eat the algae that grows in the lake and to lay their eggs.

Van Breugel and Dickinson examined the flies they caught using high-powered microscopes. They discovered that alkali flies are much hairier than most other insects. The scientists also learned that all those hairs are coated with a super water-repellent wax. The wax and hairs work together to help keep the flies dry and to create their protective bubbles.

Surrounded by swarms of alkali flies, scientist Michael Dickinson uses nets to capture some to use in laboratory experiments.

Exactly how do these bubble suits form? To find out, the scientists filmed flies diving into water collected from Mono Lake. Played at slow speed, the videos revealed that an alkali fly first pushes down on the water's surface, usually with its head. This creates a depression—a dip—in the surface. As the fly keeps pushing, the dip gets deeper and deeper until—*zip*—an air pocket forms, instantly encasing the fly in a silvery, body-hugging bubble.

Since bubbles rise and the flies want to go down, they enter the water at the lake's edge and crawl along the bottom to descend into deeper water. "The flies have long 'ninja-like' claws, which they use like grappling hooks to grab onto the rocks as they crawl in," Dickinson said.

Safe inside their bubble suits, alkali flies can stay submerged for about fifteen minutes. Returning to the surface is a snap. The flies simply let go of whatever they are gripping. Their bubbles break as they hit the surface, allowing the flies to buzz away, dry as the California desert.

CHAPTER 5
MASQUERADE

Can you spot the cuttlefish (Sepia officinalis) hiding in plain sight? Hint: The small, dark, wavy line is its eye.

NINJA SKILL
HENSO-JUTSU

WEARING A DISGUISE AND IMPERSONATING SOMEONE ELSE TO FOOL AN ENEMY OR GAIN AN ADVANTAGE

The cuttlefish glides through the water. Its smooth, soft body and wriggling arms are as pale as the sand below. Then the sand changes to gravel. The cuttlefish settles on the bottom, and instantly, it changes. Its smooth skin becomes bumpy and spotted in shades of white, brown, and gray. The disguise is so good that it's as if the cuttlefish has *become* the gravel.

Ninja were well known for wearing disguises and impersonating other people such as monks, merchants, farmers, and priests. This ninja skill was known as *henso-jutsu*. It wasn't simply about looking like someone else. It involved behaving like that person too.

Cuttlefish are masters of disguise. In a fraction of a second, they can change the color, pattern, and texture of their skin to blend in with their surroundings.

Recently, scientists learned that pharaoh cuttlefish (*Sepia pharaonis*) take camouflage to a new level. They don't just change their appearance to match their background. They can transform themselves to look remarkably like hermit crabs. They even act like hermit crabs, wiggling their "eyestalks" and scuttling along the bottom on "legs" like crabs do.

The pharaoh cuttlefish's hermit crab impersonation may be one of the best examples of *henso-jutsu* in nature. And it was discovered by chance.

THE SCIENCE BEHIND THE STORY

Kohei Okamoto had never seen anything like it. Working in the laboratory at the University of the Ryukyus in Okinawa, Japan, the scientist had just put several dozen pharaoh cuttlefish into a large tank. As he watched, some of the cuttlefish changed their appearance dramatically. They went from looking like cuttlefish to looking and acting like hermit crabs.

Okamoto and his colleagues decided to investigate. They placed new groups of pharaoh cuttlefish in tanks equipped with

Above: A *pharaoh cuttlefish* (Sepia pharaonis) *imitates a hermit crab in a tank in Okamoto's laboratory. Below: A hermit crab, just being itself.*

underwater cameras. After filming for several days, the scientists studied the video recordings. They discovered that the cuttlefish tended to impersonate hermit crabs in two different situations: in large tanks with lots of wide-open space and in smaller tanks with fish present for the cuttlefish to eat.

The scientists hypothesized that the cuttlefish might have felt exposed in the large tank, having nothing to hide behind in such a big open space. Perhaps they adopted their hermit crab disguise to make themselves look less appetizing to potential predators. (There weren't any predators in the tank, but the cuttlefish didn't know that.) A predator that would love to eat a soft, tender cuttlefish might not want to bother with a crunchy, hard-shelled crab.

The scientists also hypothesized that in the smaller tank, the cuttlefish might have impersonated hermit crabs to improve their chances of catching the fish. Hermit crabs aren't predators (they eat mostly algae and the remains of dead things), so fish aren't afraid to

A cuttlefish snags dinner using two long tentacles, which are usually kept tucked up close to the cuttlefish's body and are hidden by the arms.

approach them. Fish fooled by a cuttlefish's hermit crab disguise might swim close enough to be easily caught.

"It would be effective for cuttlefish to use multiple behavioral tactics, because that makes it difficult for their opponents—both predators and prey—to take countermeasures," said Okamoto. Then again, pharaoh cuttlefish may impersonate hermit crabs for entirely different reasons. Okamoto and his colleagues need to conduct more experiments to find out for sure.

CHAPTER 6
STUN GUNS

Viewed from the front, this bombardier beetle (Brachinus alternans) looks harmless enough. But beware of the back end . . .

NINJA SKILL
KAYAKU-JUTSU

USING DIFFERENT TYPES OF EXPLOSIVES TO DISTRACT OR DEFEAT OPPONENTS

The toad peers out from its hiding place. A beetle is approaching. And it's the perfect size for a midnight snack.

As the beetle ambles within reach, the toad darts out to snag it with its sticky tongue.

But the beetle is faster. *Psst-psst-psst-psst!* A stinky, boiling hot spray comes pulsing out of the beetle's rear end, hitting the toad square in the face.

Blinded and gagging, the toad stumbles backward. The beetle simply strolls on.

Ninja warriors used gunpowder and other explosives to escape or combat their enemies. They would have been very impressed by what bombardier beetles can do. These insects are armed with an explosive weapon—a sort of chemical machine gun—hidden in their backside.

Inside its abdomen, a bombardier beetle has a pair of structures, each with two separate compartments. One compartment contains most of the chemicals needed to create the beetle's explosive spray. The second compartment holds chemicals that get the explosion going.

When a bombardier beetle is bothered, a little flap between the two compartments opens. Chemicals from the first compartment mix with those in the second. There, the chemicals react violently to form a hot, toxic liquid. This explosive mixing of chemicals occurs repeatedly in a very short time, resulting in rapid-fire pulses of boiling-hot spray that blast out of the beetle's rear. This pulsed spray is so nasty that it stops most attackers dead in their tracks.

Another species of bombardier beetle, Stenaptinus insignis, fires its chemical blaster.

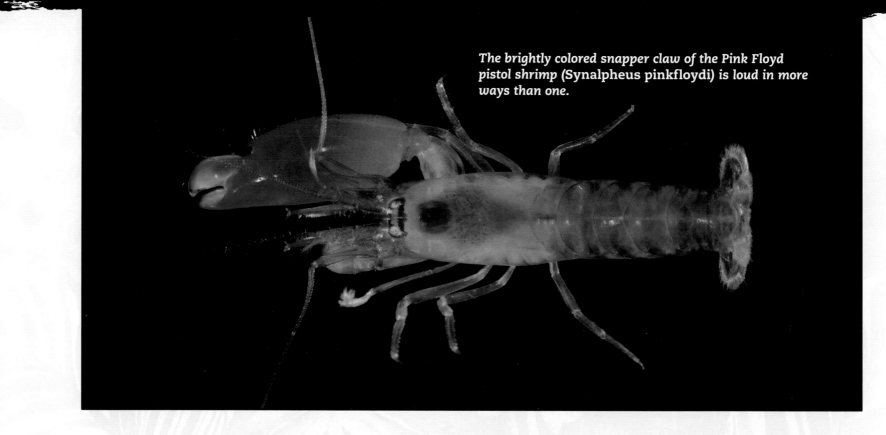

The brightly colored snapper claw of the Pink Floyd pistol shrimp (Synalpheus pinkfloydi) is loud in more ways than one.

The Pink Floyd pistol shrimp (*Synalpheus pinkfloydi*) is another animal ninja equipped with an explosive weapon. Unlike the bombardier beetle's chemical blaster, this weapon is powered by sound.

The scientists who recently discovered this little shrimp named it after the rock band Pink Floyd. The band was famous for very loud concerts.

Sound is measured in decibels. The sound of rock concerts such as those Pink Floyd performed typically measure around 120 decibels. The sound of a roaring jet engine registers about 140 decibels, while a gunshot is roughly 150 decibels.

The Pink Floyd pistol shrimp is a lot louder. It can create an explosive sound that measures an incredible 210 decibels. At close range, that's loud enough to stun—and even kill—small fish.

How does a little shrimp pull off such a big *kayaku-jutsu* trick? Pistol shrimp have two front claws. One is a small pincer. The other is a colossal snapper. The Pink Floyd's snapper claw is a neon-bright reddish pink.

When this big claw snaps shut, it does so with tremendous force and speed. Water jets out so fast that something scientists call a cavitation bubble forms near the claw's tip. This bubble exists for only a split second. When it collapses, it produces AN EXTREMELY LOUD SOUND. It also briefly generates a temperature of nearly 8,000°F (4,427°C).

If you're small enough and close enough, the Pink Floyd's snap will knock you out cold.

CHAPTER 7

THE TIES THAT BIND

Having tied up its spider prey with fine strands of sticky silk (look closely), this ground spider delivers a final, fatal bite.

NINJA SKILL

KYOKETSU-SHOGE-JUTSU

USING A *KYOKETSU-SHOGE*—A LONG, ROPELIKE WEAPON—TO TIE UP AND OVERPOWER AN OPPONENT FROM A DISTANCE

The contestants face off. In one corner, a ground spider: sturdy, burly, and low slung. In the other corner, a web-spinning spider: agile, long legs, and big fangs.

The ground spider feints forward and retreats, sizing up its opponent. Then it springs. In a blur of movement, the ground spider loops strands of sticky silk around and around the web spinner's legs. Tripping it. Trussing it up. And tying those big fangs together.

Dinner is served.

Earth is home to at least twenty-two hundred species of ground spiders. They belong to the scientific family Gnaphosidae (nah-FOHS-ih-dee). Ground spiders don't build webs to catch food. They are free-roaming predators that hunt their prey on the ground. They ambush them or chase them down and fight face-to-face.

These contests can be dangerous for the ground spiders because they don't hesitate to take on brawny beetles, muscular ants, or other types of spiders. Such opponents can fight back with powerful jaws and poisonous bites.

Yet ground spiders have a weapon that gives them an advantage. Like ninja using *kyoketsu-shoge*, these fearsome, eight-legged hunters use sticky strands of silk to tie up and immobilize their prey. And they do it with breathtaking speed.

THE SCIENCE BEHIND THE STORY

Jonas Wolff from Australia's Macquarie University is a spider expert. He wanted to learn more about how ground spiders subdue dangerous prey.

Working with colleagues from several European countries, Wolff carried out experiments using *Drassodex heeri*, a large species of ground spider. In the laboratory, the scientists placed a high-speed video camera under a container with a clear bottom. Then they put a *D. heeri* into the container with another type of spider and filmed the action from below.

By replaying videos of multiple attacks at slow speed, frame by frame, the scientists saw how these ground spiders battle their opponents.

All spiders produce silk from glands in their abdomen. Silk leaves a spider's body as fine strands that flow out of spinnerets near the abdomen's tip. Different types of silk glands make different kinds of silk. Wolff and his team discovered that *D. heeri* and other ground spiders use a strong, stretchy silk produced in their piriform (PEER-ih-form) glands for subduing prey. Web-spinning spiders produce only small amounts of this silk, usually to secure their webs to a support. But most ground spiders have huge piriform glands that produce lots of this silk. Each

These are the spinnerets of a female eastern parson spider (Herpyllus ecclesiasticus), a ground spider in the Gnaphosidae family.

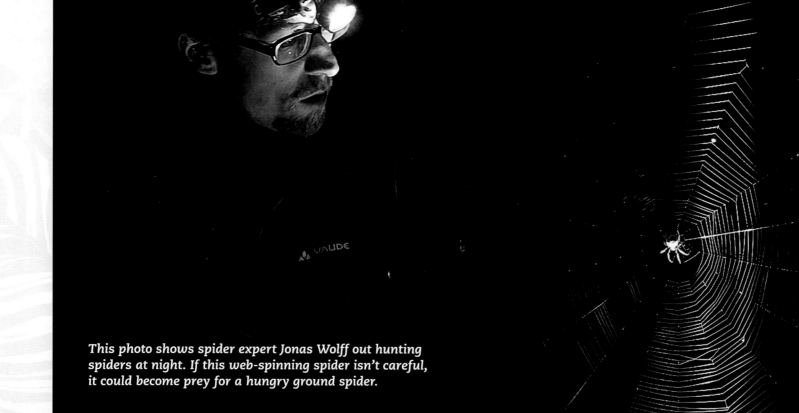

This photo shows spider expert Jonas Wolff out hunting spiders at night. If this web-spinning spider isn't careful, it could become prey for a hungry ground spider.

strand is also coated with an exceptionally tough, sticky glue that dries very fast.

When a ground spider attacks another spider, it first attaches a strand of piriform silk to the ground, like an anchor. Then it runs around, speedily flinging and looping more strands of this sticky silk around its opponent. In seconds the other spider is tied up so tightly it can't move.

Although this spider version of a *kyoketsu-shoge* is incredibly effective, it's not foolproof. "Attacking other spiders is a very risky business, and sometimes the ground spiders get bitten and paralyzed themselves," said Wolff. Nevertheless, ground spiders typically emerge triumphant in these competitions, thanks to their super-sticky, silk-slinging skills.

CHAPTER 8

SECRET AGENTS

At first glance, it is hard to tell the difference between this rove beetle (right) from Malaysia and its army ant host.

NINJA SKILL
CHOHO

SPYING—INFILTRATING AN ENEMY'S CAMP OR SOCIETY WITHOUT BEING DISCOVERED

The army ants are on the march. Hundreds of thousands swarm across the forest floor.

Spies march alongside them. The spies are rove beetles that look like ants, and their disguise is really good.

Their disguise is so good, in fact, that the ants don't notice these impostors living among them. Not even when the spies eat the ants' kids.

Army ants live in hot, humid regions around the globe. They often travel in teeming hordes that can be millions strong. And hidden among their ranks are sneaky rove beetles, *choho* masters of the insect world.

Certain species of rove beetles specialize in infiltrating army ant colonies. They look and behave remarkably like the army ants they live with. They even smell like them. If these rove beetles were human, they would make outstanding ninja spies.

The beetles gain a lot from their trickery. They live protected in ant colonies that few predators dare to attack. They feast on food that army ant soldiers bring back to the nest. And given the chance, they dine on army ant larvae too.

THE SCIENCE BEHIND THE STORY

Joseph Parker has traveled the world looking for rove beetles. A biologist from the California Institute of Technology, he's spent countless hours following columns of army ants in search of rove beetles marching among them.

It's no easy task. Rove beetles that have evolved to live with army ants are some of the rarest insects in the world. And because the beetles so closely resemble the ants they live with, they're exceedingly hard to spot.

Over the years, though, Parker has gotten very good at it. "After you have seen hundreds of thousands of ants run past, the beetles break the pattern just enough," he said. "They are often a slightly different size, shape, or color, and they sometimes walk differently than the ants."

Above: This illustration shows nine different types of rove beetles from around the world that look (and act and smell) like their army ant hosts. Below: A column of army ants marches across a fallen branch in the Amazon rain forest of Peru.

These army ants have managed to climb aboard scientist Joseph Parker as he searches for new species of rove beetles.

Many of the rove beetle species Parker and his colleagues have collected are new to science. "For me, finding these beetles is the equivalent of discovering treasure," said Parker. "After locating an ant colony and patiently waiting by the trail or excavating a nest, finding a beetle in amongst the ant chaos gives you an immense sense of success."

There is much that scientists still don't know about these extraordinary beetles. For instance, do they spend their entire lives inside army ant colonies? Where and how do they raise their young? And . . . do the ants ever discover the spies living among them? Parker hopes to find answers to these and many other questions as he and his colleagues continue their research.

CHAPTER 9
ESCAPE ARTIST

This recently discovered species of fish-scale gecko (Geckolepis megalepis) has a ninja-worthy strategy to avoid being caught.

NINJA SKILL

INTON-JUTSU

THE ART OF CONCEALMENT AND ESCAPE; BEING GOOD AT HIDING AS WELL AS GETTING AWAY

The gecko creeps along a tree branch in search of dinner. Tasty insects buzz and hum in the leafy greenness all around. Then the branch quivers ever so slightly. Before the gecko has a chance to move, the snake that's been stalking it strikes.

The snake's jaws close on the gecko's big, crunchy scales—but not the gecko. Because the little lizard has slipped out of its skin and gotten away.

A close-up of the remarkably large scales of the fish-scale gecko, Geckolepis megalepis.

The world is home to more than fifteen hundred species of geckos. Some types are quite common. But fish-scale geckos are not. They live only on the island nations of Madagascar and Comoros, off Africa's southeastern coast.

True to their name, fish-scale geckos have large scales that overlap like scales on a fish. The scales, tinted in browns and grays, provide great camouflage. But the scales are special for another reason. They come off at the slightest touch, along with the underlying skin. As uncomfortable as that sounds, the process is bloodless. And the scales grow back.

Inton-jutsu is sometimes called the ninja art of "disappearing." When it comes to making a ninja-like escape, being able to leave replaceable pieces of yourself behind is quite a talent.

THE SCIENCE BEHIND THE STORY

In 2017 scientists described a new species of fish-scale gecko in northern Madagascar. Mark Scherz, from Ludwig Maximilian University in Munich, Germany, was part of the team. The scientists named their discovery *Geckolepis megalepis*, which means "scaled gecko with very large scales." It's a good name, because the scales of *G. megalepis* are larger than those of any other known gecko.

G. megalepis and other fish-scale geckos are unusual in that they can shed scales easily and instantly to escape a predator's grip. "Scales and the top layer of skin (the epidermis) come off in more or less one chunk," said Scherz. Wherever scales have been lost, the skin beneath looks pink, shiny, and a tad slimy. A bit like skin under a freshly picked scab.

Lost scales grow back in a process called regeneration, which Scherz and his colleagues think takes about two to three weeks. The geckos probably hide in a sheltered place while the missing scales regrow. When regeneration is complete, their scaly body covering is as good as new.

Can *G. megalepis* and other fish-scale geckos regenerate lost scales indefinitely? "As far as we know—yes," said Scherz. "The skin heals without a trace of scars." That means *G. megalepis* and other fish-scale geckos can make their ninja-like escapes again and again and again . . .

This **G. megalepis** *shed a large portion of its scales to pull off a successful escape. When the scales grow back, there won't even be a scar.*

MEET THE SCIENTISTS

Many thanks to the scientists who shared their insights, generously answered my questions, and reviewed relevant sections of the text. Those featured in this book are

Michael H. Dickinson
California Institute of Technology
Pasadena, California

Robert J. Full
University of California at Berkeley
Berkeley, California

Kohei Okamoto
University of the Ryukyus
Okinawa, Japan

Joseph Parker
California Institute of Technology
Pasadena, California

Mark D. Scherz
Ludwig Maximilian University of Munich
Munich, Germany

Hannah Sheppard-Brennand
Southern Cross University
Coffs Harbour, New South Wales, Australia

Floris van Breugel
University of Nevada
Reno, Nevada

Alexander Wilson
University of Plymouth
Plymouth, Devon, England

Jonas O. Wolff
Macquarie University
Sydney, New South Wales, Australia

AUTHOR'S NOTE

The idea that sparked this book came when I read an article about Hannah Sheppard-Brennand's discovery that the sea urchin *Tripneustes gratilla* releases pedicellaria heads as defensive weapons. The images of the tiny, triangular heads instantly brought to mind ninja throwing stars. Once I started researching ninja weapons and skills, potential candidates for other animal ninja seemed to pop up everywhere. The truth is that animal ninja are plentiful and those featured in this book are just a small sampling of what nature has to offer. It's also true that words alone cannot capture the wonder of seeing sailfish corral a school of sardines, a bombardier beetle deploy its chemical blaster, a gecko grip an impossibly smooth surface, or any of the other adaptations highlighted in the text. For that reason, I encourage readers to watch the videos listed under "More to Explore" on page 47.

One of the most rewarding aspects of writing nonfiction is what I learn while doing the research. I discovered that the history of the ninja in Japanese culture spans many centuries and that ninjutsu is much more than the martial arts moves we often see in movies and on television. Ninja weapons and skills evolved over time, driven largely by the need for stealth, concealment, and speed of action in defending against more powerful, better-equipped opponents. From a biologist's perspective, that is not so very different from the way in which natural selection works to shape the remarkable adaptations of the animals, plants, and other living things with which we share this planet.

I am grateful to the scientists whose kind assistance made this book possible. Their passion for their work was an inspiration, and I hope that some of my readers may ultimately follow in their footsteps—or even become their graduate students! It's always encouraging, as a writer, to have scientists say they like the idea behind a book. So when Kohei Okamoto wrote in an early email that he was delighted to learn I was using the behavior of pharaoh cuttlefish as an example of a ninja-worthy disguise, I was thrilled. When he later told me he was born and raised near Iga, a city famous for ninja in Japan, I felt this book was meant to be. Finally, a special thanks to 15th Dan Shihan Dr. Michael Asuncion, martial arts master and head of the Michigan Bujinkan Dojo in Ann Arbor, for reviewing the text and helping me write accurately and authentically about the art of the ninja.

GLOSSARY

algae: found mostly in water, a diverse group of organisms that uses energy from sunlight to manufacture food (photosynthesis). Some types of algae consist of a single cell, while others, such as seaweeds, have many cells.

alkaline: a chemical term used to describe something that is basic (the opposite of acidic)

ecologist: a scientist who primarily studies relationships between living things and their environments

evolve: to change over time through natural processes

exoskeleton: the tough, often rigid body covering of animals such as crabs, shrimp, spiders, and many insects

forceps: a pair of pincers or tweezers that scientists use when examining living things

hypothesize: to suggest a hypothesis—a possible scientific explanation—for something discovered or observed

impersonate: to look and act like something else to fool someone or avoid being noticed

infiltrate: to sneak into

larvae: the young forms of certain types of animals, including many insects, that hatch from eggs and later change into very different looking adult forms. Just one is a larva.

masquerade: the wearing of a disguise

pedicellariae: small, stalked structures topped with pincerlike jaws found at the base of sea urchin spines. Just one is a pedicellaria.

predator: an animal that captures and eats other animals

prey: an animal that is captured and eaten by predators

semiautonomous: acting independently to some degree

setae: microscopic hairs on a gecko's toe pads. Just one is a seta.

spatulae: the fine, hairlike "split ends" of setae. Just one is a spatula.

species: a specific kind of living thing

spinneret: a spider's silk-spinning organ

van der Waals forces: weak attractive forces between atoms and molecules

venomous: poisonous

SOURCE NOTES

9 Robert Full, e-mail communication with the author, July 23, 2018.

13 Hannah Sheppard-Brennand, e-mail communication with the author, July 11, 2018.

13 Sheppard-Brennand.

13 Sheppard-Brennand.

17 Alexander Wilson, e-mail communication with the author, August 6, 2018.

17 Wilson.

21 Michael Dickinson, e-mail communication with the author, July 27, 2018.

25 Kohei Okamoto, e-mail communication with the author, July 27, 2018.

33 Jonas Wolff, e-mail communication with the author, July 27, 2018.

36 Joseph Parker, e-mail communication with the author, July 30, 2018.

37 Parker.

41 Mark Scherz, e-mail communication with the author, July 27, 2018.

41 Scherz.

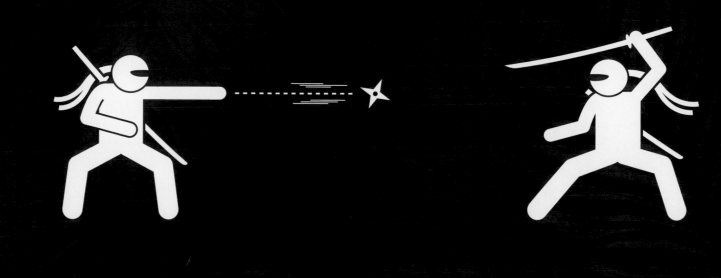

SELECTED BIBLIOGRAPHY

You can find the complete bibliography of sources that I consulted for this book at http://www.rebeccajohnsonbooks.com.

Herbert-Read, James E., Pawel Romanczuk, Stefan Krause, Daniel Strömbom, Pierre Couillaud, Paolo Domenici, Ralf H. J. M. Kurvers, Stefano Marras, John F. Steffensen, Alexander D. M. Wilson, and Jens Krause. "Proto-cooperation: Group Hunting Sailfish Improve Hunting Success by Alternating Attacks on Grouping Prey." *Proceedings of the Royal Society B* 283, no. 1842 (November 16, 2016). https://doi.org/10.1098/rspb.2016.1671.

Maruyama, Munetoshi, and Joseph Parker. "Deep-Time Convergence in Rove Beetle Symbionts of Army Ants." *Current Biology* 27, no. 6 (March 20, 2017): 920–926. https://doi.org/10.1016/j.cub.2017.02.030.

Okamoto, Kohei, Haruhiko Yasumuro, Akira Mori, and Yuzuru Ikeda. "Unique Arm-Flapping Behavior of the Pharaoh Cuttlefish, *Sepia pharaonis*: Putative Mimicry of a Hermit Crab." *Journal of Ethology* 35, no. 3 (September 2017): 307–311. https://doi.org/10.1007/s10164-017-0519-7.

Scherz, Mark D., J. D. Daza, J. Köhler, M. Vences, and F. Glaw. "Off the Scale: A New Species of Fish-Scale Gecko (Squamata: Gekkonidae: *Geckolepis*) with Exceptionally Large Scales." *PeerJ* 5: e2955 (February 7, 2017). https://doi.org/10.7717/peerj.2955.

Sheppard-Brennand, Hannah, Alistair G. B. Poore, and Symon A. Dworjanyn. "A Waterborne Pursuit-Deterrent Signal Deployed by a Sea Urchin." *American Naturalist* 189, no. 6 (June 2017): 700–708. https://doi.org/10.1086/691437.

Van Breugel, Floris, and Michael H. Dickinson. "Superhydrophobic Diving Flies (*Ephydra hians*) and the Hypersaline Waters of Mono Lake." PNAS 114, no. 51 (December 19, 2017): 13483–13488. https://doi.org/10.1073/pnas.1714874114.

Wolff, Jonas O., Milan Řezáč, Tomáš Krejči, and Stanislav N. Gorb. "Hunting with Sticky Tape: Functional Shift in Silk Glands of Araneophagous Ground Spiders (Gnaphosidae)." *Journal of Experimental Biology* 220, no. 12 (June 15, 2017): 2250–2259. https://doi.org/10.1242/jeb.154682.

MORE TO EXPLORE

Books

Hirsch, Rebecca E. *When Plants Attack: Strange and Terrifying Plants*. Minneapolis: Millbrook Press, 2019.

Johnson, Rebecca L. *Masters of Disguise: Amazing Animal Tricksters*. Minneapolis: Millbrook Press, 2016.

Johnson, Rebecca L. *When Lunch Fights Back: Wickedly Clever Animal Defenses*. Minneapolis: Millbrook Press, 2015.

Videos

"Alkali Flies of Mono Lake"
https://youtu.be/Qt_0DxOLbQU
Michael Dickinson narrates this video of bubble-encased alkali flies in Mono Lake that features lab experiments showing how the flies enter the water.

"The Bombardier Beetle's Chemical Blaster"
https://www.youtube.com/watch?v=TgqF-ND2XcY
Here you can see a video of a bombardier beetle firing its weapon from the outside as well as a high-speed X-ray imaging video of the weapon firing inside the beetle's body.

"Cuttlefish Mimicking Hermit Crabs"
https://www.youtube.com/watch?v=IgwWJEA67Ls
This video shows pharaoh cuttlefish imitating hermit crabs in the laboratory at Japan's University of the Ryukyus.

"Gecko Toes, or May the Force Be with You"
https://www.youtube.com/watch?v=YeSuQm7KfaE
This short, animated video provides a cleverly illustrated explanation of van Der Waals forces, the secret to the gecko's grip.

"Ground Spider vs. Giant House Spider"
https://www.facebook.com/AusSMC/videos/951812798291868/
Taken by Jonas Wolff, this video—slowed down ten times—shows a *Drassodex heeri* ground spider capturing a house spider using its sticky silk.

"Sailfish Attacking Bait Ball of Sardines"
https://youtu.be/VISEHbpHkn4?t=2
Dive into the water with Alexander Wilson and his scientist team as they film hunting sailfish in action off Mexico's coast.

INDEX

PHOTO ACKNOWLEDGMENTS

Image credits: Backgrounds: Natallia Novik/Shutterstock.com; Miloje/Shutterstock.com. Content: CathyKeife/iStock/Getty Images, p. 1; © David Welling/naturepl.com, p. 2; Fotokvadrat/Shutterstock.com, p. 4; © Pictures from History/Bridgeman Images, p. 5; © Michael D. Kern/naturepl.com, p. 6; Leremy/Shutterstock.com, pp. 7, 11, 15, 19, 23, 31, 35, 39; POWER AND SYRED/ SCIENCE PHOTO LIBRARY/Getty Images, p. 8 (top); Andrew Syred/Science Source, p. 8 (bottom); Laura Westlund/Independent Picture Service, pp. 9, 12; © Becca Saunders/Minden Pictures, p. 10; © Hannah Sheppard-Brennand, p. 13, 42 (right second from top); Rodrigo Friscione/Image Source/Getty Images, p. 14; Nature Picture Library/Alamy Stock Photo, p. 16; Reinhard Dirscherl/ Alamy Stock Photo, p. 17; © Floris van Breugel, pp. 18, 21, 42 (right third from top); © Wild Wonders of Europe/Pitkin/NPL/ Minden Pictures, p. 22; © Kohei Okamoto, p. 24 (top), 42 (left third from top); Pablo Zgraggen/EyeEm/Getty Images, p. 24; Sompraaong0042/Shutterstock.com, p. 25; johannviloria/Shutterstock.com, p. 26; © Satoshi Kuribayashi/Minden Pictures, p. 28; Arthur Anker/Oxford University Museum of Natural History/Wikimedia Commons (CC BY 3.0), p. 29; © Arno Grabolle, p. 30; Glen Peterson/Wikimedia Commons (CC BY 3.0), p. 32; Courtesy of Jonas Wolff, pp. 33, 42 (right bottom); © Joseph Parker, pp. 34, 36 (top), 36 (bottom), 37, 42 (left bottom); Frank Glaw, pp. 38, 40, 41; Courtesy of Mark Scherz, p. 42 (top right).

Cover: © Piotr Naskrecki/Minden Pictures (gecko); Natallia Novik/Shutterstock.com.

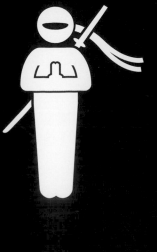